Your Skin Is A Country

Your Skin
Is A
Country

POEMS BY NORA MITCHELL

Alice James Books
Cambridge • Massachusetts

Library of Congress Cataloging-in-Publication Data
Mitchell, Nora, 1956 –
I. Your Skin Is A Country.
PS3563.I78Y68 1988   811'.54 88-14632
ISBN 0-914086-82-0 (cloth)
ISBN 0-914086-83-9 (paper)

Printed in the United States of America
This book has been set in Baskerville by Barbara Levy
Cover illustration and design by Nora Mitchell

ACKNOWLEDGMENTS

I would like to acknowledge the following publications in which some of these poems, or earlier versions of them, first appeared: *Calyx* ("Bells Off San Salvador," "Driving to Florida with a Parrot in the Back," "The Ghost on Chocorua," "Ursa Major"); *Dark Horse* ("The Reed"); *Hawaii Review* ("Stars Sleep on Cheju Island"); *Kether* ("Blueberries," "From This Kitchen," "From a Watercolor by Pissarro"); *The Nantucket Review* ("Collagen"); *Ploughshares* ("Replay"); *Shadowgraphs* ("Immigrants"); *Sojourner* ("Ladders," "My Bones Sing," "The Red Sea"). Three poems also appeared in an anthology, *Witness and Wait: Thirteen Poets From New England* (Every Other Thursday Press, 1988).

The epigraphs come from the following poems: "A Smile" by Kim Chi-ha, translated by David R. McCann, and "White Deer Lake" by Chŏng Chi-yong, translated by Peter H. Lee. Both poems are included in the collection, *The Silence of Love: Twentieth-Century Korean Poetry*, edited and with an introduction by Peter H. Lee (The University Press of Hawaii, 1980).

The publication of this book was made possible with support from the Massachusetts Council on the Arts and Humanities, a state agency whose funds are recommended by the Governor and appropriated by the State Legislature.

Alice James Books are published by the
Alice James Poetry Cooperative, Inc.

Alice James Books
33 Richdale Avenue
Cambridge, MA 02140

Emily Skoler

CONTENTS

ONE

Swimming Where the Mississippi and Missouri Meet   *3*
Los Angeles   *4*
Blueberries   *6*
Aubade   *7*
Driving to Florida with a Parrot in the Back   *8*
From this Kitchen   *9*
Particles   *10*
Replay   *11*
Colleen   *13*
Wisteria   *14*
The Reed   *16*
Lullaby   *18*
Collagen   *19*
Running into a Star   *20*
The Red Sea   *21*
Half Life   *22*
Ursa Major   *24*
Exposure   *27*

TWO

The Forgetting of Napalm   *31*
The Ghost on Chocorua   *32*
Bells off San Salvador   *34*
Meditation on TV   *36*
The Road from Inch'ŏn   *37*
The Colors of Mourning   *38*
Sunset over the Yellow Sea   *39*
The Women Divers of Cheju-do   *41*
Stars Sleep on Cheju Island   *43*

THREE

Ladders	*47*
On Lakeview Avenue	*48*
Red Eyes and Teeth	*49*
The Locker Room	*50*
Letter to my Daughter	*51*
My Bones Sing	*52*
Pine Down	*54*
Kudzu	*55*
Baboon Heart	*56*
Faggots	*57*
From a Watercolor by Pissarro	*58*
Deer at Night	*59*
Nocturne	*60*
Immigrants	*61*

ONE

SWIMMING WHERE THE MISSISSIPPI
AND MISSOURI MEET

In high school we all swam
where the Missouri and the Mississippi meet,
at the point where the currents cross,
where the rivers, as one river
could turn suddenly and seize my legs,
huge hands and muddy knuckles wrapped
around my calves and thighs, cramping the muscles,
hauling me under, only to let me go finally in a new place.

We were crazy with summer and beer,
living for those moments when we burst
to the surface and heard voices yelling.
I would break back to the air scared as I could be,
light and mud in my eyes and my lungs full of pins
        and fists.
I could feel the river shrug me off and turn away.

Feeling you roll towards the far side of the bed,
panic grips my legs at night.
I kick inside my shell of sleep and wake you.
When we come back up to the surface,
for a second I am in a place
I do not know. Your skin, near as the water,
floats calm and sure beneath my fingers.

LOS ANGELES

The queens sing themselves to sleep,
arms crossed over their flat, flat chests.
If I were a man I would join them,
teasing the straight young men
whose eyes cloud with confusion and desire.
At night before I slept
I would palm my own flat chest,
knowing that my secret lay there
on that expanse, taut as the sheets on my made-up bed,
tempting as the empty parking lot
at a mall on Sunday morning
to a teenager in a fast car.
A real man, I would kiss the boys and make them cry —
all the boys passing through my hands
and vanishing into the blue.

Over the Western sea the sun sinks
and the clouds pile up.
To live on the edge of this continent
makes the skin crawl over my bones.
The U.S. runs out here
on a dizzy, deserted beach and there's no telling
what slides into the sea in the dark.

But I'm neither a man, nor a queen
who wants the slim-hipped boys.
I want the slim-hipped women,
the ones who pass
for adolescent boys in the streets at night,
and the lush women, who move with the sure

gliding delight that they've got
silk between their legs and thunder
clustered on their tongues.
If I had breasts like theirs, I'd sleep
with one arm curved across my chest.

Over the Western sea the sun vanishes into the blue.
To live on this continent exhilarates me:
there's no telling
what the land becomes in the dark.

BLUEBERRIES

It's too bad you don't,
but I like them.
Small and round,
they feel good in my mouth.
Sometimes even hard,
they're best right off the bush
hot as sunlight.
At the center there's grit.
Clams, mussels, oysters
all have dirt inside,
something to bite down on.
Sometimes our teeth hit.
Harsh as a word like bitch,
a stone lying between your breasts,
our words become small and round,
even hard,
but inside your mouth
it's all soft
I know.

AUBADE

The car picks up and the radio sings.
It's five a.m. and we never went to bed.
You say, I'll talk and you drive.
The steering wheel feels like a wheel of power.
The streets are ours from Charlestown to Quincy.
The sun comes up behind buildings and gas tanks.
At six you're falling asleep.
I want to wake you and say, see, see,
but your head rolls just a little
with the turning of the wheel.
The sun is white and huge.
There's more traffic and you're asleep.
It's past six and I think of going home.
You said, I'll talk, you drive.
I can't remember what you said, nor what I answered.

The car is fast on near-empty streets.
At redlights I slow down, look, then go.

DRIVING TO FLORIDA
WITH A PARROT IN THE BACK

First you make your mouth a tunnel
and remember all the things
that have run through you.
In the back of the car the parrot talks to itself.
In the front we're silent.
Sometimes I loosen your right hand
from the wheel and hold it.
We brought the parrot along
like a canary carried into the coal mines.
Driving long distance
is like being in a tunnel —
the highway has walls, a roof.
Sunlit exits flash by
and the car is a shadow that grows,
shrinks, and grows. The exits beckon,
squares of light. Off the highway
the world is rich and appealing.
Life in the middle of America
looks easy. We could stop, part,
leave the parrot in an airtight car,
get jobs, get married to steady men,
raise the babies we both want.
But we only stop at rest areas and gas stations.
By nightfall we circle
Washington's outskirts, a ribbon of industry:
lights reflected on water, steam,
the smell of chemicals.
I watch the dashboard, the orange
needle of speed. As cars pass,
I glance at the parrot. We hover,
my heart contracts.

FROM THIS KITCHEN

I roll on the floor.
The linoleum tiles ripple
like the wheat of your laughter.

You lean against the stove.
Nothing out of the ordinary,
the light is losing its color

and my eyes fail to adjust.
Dust sticks to my sweater
and the wheat goes still.

Lights blink in the distance.
There are oil derricks
rising from the prairie.

The pumps run all night;
men swarm over the rigs.
You stand above me

and I can smell you close.
From this kitchen the world is not so distant.
Your face turns male, then back.

Your mother is in prison again
and you shave your legs for work.
The hairs grow back in winter.

Someone tries to call on the telephone
and the record ends.
In the silence you whisper I want you.

PARTICLES

After I leave her I lie down on her lawn
and wonder what to do next.
Stretched out, I stare at the sky.
In all that daylight
I feel dark inside and close my eyes.
Through my shirt I feel the dirt,
the small stones and roots.
My breath moves the length of my body.
It reaches the base of my spine and warms my gut.
I am clean, I let it clean me out.
My vertebrae nestle into the grass
like a flock of sparrows
disappearing into a field.
My palms and fingers go flat and still.
I imagine her at one of the windows above me,
lifting a curtain, staring down,
and seeing nothing.
At night the lights from her house
will tumble out onto the lawn
in rectangular patches,
until, one by one, she extinguishes the lamps,
leaving a single bulb high up.
That will be her, burning in sleep.

REPLAY

for Judy Couffer, 1955-1986

All afternoon I try not
to watch the shuttle explode.
On silent televisions throughout the hospital
it lifts, a compact shining house
astride a column of flame, curves,
and blows apart, each piece
leaving its trail of smoke as it
dives for the sea. Again
and again, the camera slides over the faces
of the families watching from the ground,
while we wait in the crowded
room for the results of the biopsy,
the doctors' final word on
the explosion in your body,
cells flung far and wide
as so many scraps of metal that still
must be dredged up from the ocean floor —
bladder, uterus, hip, lymph.
And unexpectedly, in the lung,
wedged among the sacs and fine-meshed
blood vessels, the delicate engines
of exchange, where poison and air
trade places — even there.
How far small things travel.
Over the weeks as submarines
and divers locate bits and pieces
of the shuttle, I wish such salvage
crews could enter the currents

of your body and extract the wreckage,
cell by cell. Instead, they load your blood
with a chemical so strong that
the night I stay over the nurses
give me rubber gloves to wear
in case I empty your bedpan,
because even the piss will burn.
I watch the replay of
the diagnosis, over and over;
under the eyelids the soft
word, malignant, bursts
into a thousand fragments,
each one a seed
repeating itself.

COLLEEN

*Shot dead while searching for the teenaged boys
who had assaulted her and a retarded man
she was accompanying*

Pressed into the spray of the shower,
I remember the shape of myself
for the first time in days.
The soap, still dry, sticks to my hand.
A piece of fishing lore from childhood
comes back to me:
though loose again in the live stream,
a fish touched by a dry hand
is already dying. Sitting
on the sidewalk beside your car,
you hold your hand
over the bullet hole in your throat.
Glass glitters on the asphalt,
caught in the lights of the street.
Neighbors run out, shouting.
I was part way through
the story in the paper
before I realized that it was you.
Bit by bit, I make the water hotter
until my skin stings.
I close my eyes, duck my head,
and imagine swimming,
my limbs loose in the stream.
Your car sits there with the door wide open,
cracked silver scales where the window was.

WISTERIA

The vine muscles its way up
from the ground and wraps
its trunk around the corner porch post.
In its wood I see narrow bodies
jumping straight against the sky,
hard, the way basketball players
turn, leap, and release the ball as soft
and loose as these light flowers hang.
Their sneakers make small, sharp

cries against the floorboards.
It's almost erotic, the way
those big-bodied men jump so high,
every muscle clenched,
then dangle mid-air with the ball
(seeming small in their big hands)
nesting for one last instant before flight.
They cradle it as tenderly as
a woman holds a man's balls in her hand.

To float like that!
At five I walked into a model heart
the size of a cozy room. In the dark
red light, anchored to a parent's hand,
I grew dizzy and drifted free,
too scared even to look for my feet.
All around me someone's heart
beat and I floated at the center
of the largest muscle in the world.

At the core of the massive glass globe,
where whispers travel across the inverted
surface and sound grows dull
at the center, I felt huge

and small, the kid in the heart grown up.
Suspended beside Africa, the continent curled
right under my feet. I kept seeing
the photographs the astronauts brought back,
tourist snapshots of the small, round ball.

When Greenland Eskimoes hunted for seal
in the deep fjords, some days grew
so still and bright that, while they floated,
waiting and motionless, they would feel themselves
start to fall. Paralyzed,
they would fall and fall into a valley of air and light.
As a child in my grandmother's house
I drifted, englobed:
her glass and wood cases overflowed

with Cherokee artifacts, arrowheads, tools,
small paint pots. She taught me to draw
and I tried the wisteria vines
and first saw the bodies there.
The wood bulged with the muscles of an arm,
the crook of a knee. With my broad
white pad flat on the porch in front of me
and the sun sliding across the floor,
I'd start to spin and the house

would tilt and the kudzu rush
forward as if to swallow us whole.
Looking close at the petals, I now expect
the whorls of fingerprints to show
in the pink, translucent flesh.
Holding them to my face or brushing by,
I'm prepared for hands to close
upon my skin, for arms to take me up;
to nest one last instant before flight.

THE REED

It is only a straw, though thinner
than the ones we were given in grade school
to drink our milk with. I test it
with care, wedge one leg
beneath a submerged log, and sink my arm
into the water to search
for roots to wrap my fingers in. Long ago,
I read this: a man makes his escape,
using a reed and a log. Far off
hounds are baying and yapping,
though there's no way to tell
just how far. I hold the reed
between my teeth and lips and push myself
down into the thick reedy water to wait.
Every once in a while I open my eyes
and peer around — at the watered down sunlight,
at the motion in a clump of roots,
wishing it still, wishing it harmless.
I feel like the troll
which lives and waits beneath the bridge,
feared by all travellers, but more afraid
of remaining under that bridge
than any passerby is scared of me.
I'm sick of waiting. I can feel my skin
sucking in the water,
giving up the fight to keep liquid out.
The hounds still sing somewhere.
My fingers look like five white minnows
hunting for food through the murk.
The cloth of my shirt floats loose,
old skin flapping.
I want to scratch it. I want to move.
I want to run on the warm, hard ground,

but I hear splashing and men's voices
and see a green rubber boot poke
through the water not far from my head.
I hold still and pull the air
inch by inch down my straw,
down my windpipe, and into my lungs,
and then push it out hard as a whisper,
the swampland breathing.

LULLABY

I stand beside the bay as it rocks itself to sleep.
Surf mutters and glows in the dark,
tumbling the soft phosphorescent

creatures of the sea (under a microscope
they become lanterns, ridged and crystalline).
I would fish them out, carry them home in my cupped
      palms,

and, singing, lie down to rest. Who knows
what the sea shakes loose in the night?
When I swim I fear the things that rise

and bump against my feet. Do bodies
wash upon the shore from nowhere,
concocted of nothing?

COLLAGEN

It is the glue: fibrous protein
lining the tissue we assume

must knit itself together, as though
by some inner gravity.

And like other things
of the body —

heart, lung, kidney,
vulnerable as small boats —

even inside, something must caulk the gaps
between the pieces. Connections

stretch tangible as threads, the jostle
of airborne dust, the delicate brush

of another's body. This air,
melted down, would yield its own answer.

RUNNING INTO A STAR

Thirty-five miles an hour
one block
from home it appears,
many-armed
star, at the center of the windshield
bursts in front of me
embedded
in the glass, where the lights
of the street catch
sign of what
when I turn off
the ignition I realize
is violence
I have been shot at, a BB aimed
into the passing
traffic, casual
I run my fingers over the mark
my dumb luck
but start to shake later

THE RED SEA

Slick and uneven, the bottom
is hard walking. The walls quiver
like vats of jelly. Inside, the fish
continue about their business
and, almost shyly, we spy on them.
The way they barrel along!
The way the sun shines in on them
as if this were a private room
and we just passersby in the road!
A child touches the left-hand wall, tries
to pluck one out. An elder
grabs her hand and we all press on.
The soft mud sucks at our feet.
We wrap cloth around our faces,
the path smells so strongly of salt
and dead sea creatures. A waste.
We step over them, the known
and unknown fish, caught
unprepared when the water drew back, left
to fall through this sudden canyon of air.

HALF LIFE

When the emergency broadcasting system
finally sounds for real
and sirens, exotic,
ungainly birds
I never noticed before, burst
into dreadful song
on the fire escapes, the people
in my city do not panic. We flow from the buildings and
flood the streets, crowding the open squares.
As I pass an office window, I see a woman
inside talking
on the telephone. She lifts
one ringed hand
in front of her
face   (somewhere in middle age, she is
pretty, but so thin
I wince)
and turns it
slowly, as if she were modeling a glove.
In the streets the people watch the sky.
Though danger may still
be hours,
or minutes,   distant, something
should show there   to prove what
is happening.
No one has any way of knowing.
But,
the crisis is averted and then we all walk home.
Unsteady
as newborn
creatures

                we are stunned to find
                            legs
                                    beneath us
                        and sidewalks, even bridges,
to walk upon.
                                            Weeks pass and
I grow used to my body again, sense, cushioned by
muscle and fat,   the long bones
of my arm, watch my   knuckles
                                    roll
                            beneath the skin.

                When the caws and screeches filled the air,
                I saw the weird birds of death rise to
            crowd the sky. I felt them swoop and dive for
                        the precious stuff
                of my eyes, remembering the horror movie of
childhood —   unable
                            to duck, or to cover; with my hands dumb
at my sides and
            my mouth still as some strange alloy,

                                the life in me tried
                                to get
                                        airborne. I tried to forget
            I ever had a body, as if
            I were one of the wild shadows, a dark v
            incised in blue.   I tried to forget

                        the bodies of those I love
            as I dove
            towards them.

                                                                    23

URSA MAJOR

One –
In the dark I hear voices and feel bodies
hands on my legs and shoulders and stomach
They touch me all over
It is all hands
Ursa, I ask myself, what is going on
I roll over someone and she laughs
Stones and roots poke into my back
I hear voices all around me
talking, moaning, singing
the noises of the subway as it rushes the station
the wind pushed through the tunnel
a truck starting on a hill, gears grinding
the whine of tires, horns, the cries of vendors
a car door slammed, the shout of hello
a backfire startling as a gunshot, the gunshot itself perhaps
children running and laughing, the dull and steady roar
All around me I hear soft voices
People in conversation
People singing
Far off there is wailing
The sound rises

Two –
I am driving through curtains of water
Truck tires throw spray into my windshield
White and red lights bob in front of me
White on the left, red on the right
The wheel comes to life in my hands
pulling right and left

Three –
I wake up with a bear staring me in the face
I hear it breathing and think I feel
its breath on my forehead
It's a shadow blocking out half the stars
Its eyes are two small lights in its black bulk
They vanish then reappear
Calm, Ursa, I say to myself, stay calm
My forehead grows cool again
I hold my breath

Four –
Color rises from the road
I am driving a wild ouija board straight into the dawn
Street signs populate my head
One reads women working
Another, no left turn
Blue lights pulse inside my wrist
Times I disappear
Times I grow so big I pass unseen
I can go anywhere
The Great Bear strolls above my bed
I cannot sleep
The stars start talking
Ursa, I coax, try to sleep

Five –
On the fringe of the railroad yard
goldenrod bends over us
pale hands of night
I lie with my lover

I touch her stomach
and the insides of her thighs
My hands dip into warm plum
Soft her name is on my tongue

Six –
I fear everything is gone and wave my hands
No, Ursa, no, no
I think again, everything is gone
All I hear are feet on pavement
the motion of bodies, cloth and flesh rubbing
We pass gutted tanks, jeeps broken and leaning
against the walls of buildings, soldiers slumped
at the wheels as if sleeping
with their helmets pulled over their eyes
The city is quiet
Broad daylight dazzles its streets
The nightwork over
I join people walking about
We survey what has been done, we do nothing else

Seven –
I wake curled up in a field of long and ragged grass
The scent of wet dirt and leaves is in my nostrils
As I move someone stirs beside me
I turn to see who lies there
The side of her face catches the early light
Her hair falls away and into the grass
The curve of her lip is beautiful
I do not know her
Gently, I shake her shoulder to wake her

EXPOSURE

As I leave the hospital, I hear
the flashbulbs crackle, the white
whine of recharging batteries.
Reporters keep asking how I feel.
The hand I lift to hide my face
may as well be transparent,
the gesture dumb and archaic,
like that of the unknowing soldier
tested with his buddies
in a desert trench. Told to duck
and close his eyes, as if in prayer,
he sees the white flash anyway, sees through
the flesh of his hands to the quick, gray bones.

The space behind his fingers
is no longer private. The space inside
his closed eyes no longer a merciful dark.

The clear round eyes blink and light floods my gut —
the folds of my bowel, the bunched liver.
My image finds temporary shelter
in all those tiny black houses.

Their doors will open later.
I will spill out
into rooms bathed in red light.

My hand hides nothing.
My emotion freezes in the doorway of the hospital,
a paper grief. I fear those pictures
will hold me in that place,
like the fourteen-year-old runaway,
who happened to be at Kent State

in May of 1970. She screams perpetually
over the fallen student and the small
river of his blood. Now that she has grown,
what does she think of that moment
when she looked up into the clear-eyed camera?
Or, the two figures falling from a hotel on fire,
who ride their mattress like a magic carpet,
caught in the camera lens, a flake of ash,
falling soft, soft, — oh, I hope — so soft.

TWO

Ah, but then I was standing,
and the grasses, left forgotten,
beneath my steps and far behind me
arose, burning white as the spirit
of the summer earth.
Bluffs, valleys, ridges — all rose up,
like a battle-cry, like fire
rose up in ecstasy.
                                        — Kim Chi-ha

THE FORGETTING OF NAPALM

She runs on a dark-wet clay road,
a child running in a photograph.
She wears no clothes, has no pubic hair,
and hangs her hands away from her body
as if she does not know what to do with them.
In the background her village burns.
I have always hoped
that after he snapped his picture, the cameraman
threw down his camera, folded her in his arms,
and listened to her cry.

The things we forget: how the leaves look
when the trees first bud.
Not by day (I remember that well enough),
but at night under a streetlight
I always forget how they turn
pale as foam, trees in flower.

Napalm is no longer in our daily talk
and some of those who did not watch each night
its dark orange blossom in Vietnamese fields and hamlets
have never heard the word at all. The fire
that clings and burns, the fire I thought
would never let us go.

Perhaps napalm does not exist
until we remember just what it was:
the gel in gasoline, its only use
to make sure things burned.
As personal as the shirt of a dead friend,
war has its intimate moments,
when the fire hugs, holds, and won't let go.

THE GHOST ON CHOCORUA

*After much fighting, the settlers pursued the last Indian
warrior, Chief Chocorua, to the top of the mountain. Rather
than let himself be captured, he threw himself from a large
outcropping on the summit. His wife's tears filled the hole his
falling body made at the foot of the mountain to form Chocorua
Lake. It is said that his ghost haunts the mountain still.*

It did not come to pass — the land
as we prayed it could be. I did not weep
to fill your grave; the earth itself grieved.
I climbed instead, with our dream,
along a streambed to the very stone
from which you threw your body.

It was despair that plucked your body
from the summit and sucked you down to land.
In my stomach you dropped like a stone,
over and over, until the thought of weeping
sickened me. Our dream
kept me fighting, despite my grief.

When you jumped, they took your courage to heart
        and grieved.
What I had left of you was just your body,
as broken as our lifelong dream.
And the settlers got the land.
When I finally wept,
I threw my tears at them like stones,

though their stories have me watering the stone
of your grave: your lady, grieving.
Had I chosen to weep,
I would have poisoned that body
of water with my salt, and the land
that rims it would be peopled only by my dreams.

Nightly, I have kept those dreams
in vigil around your stone.
By day I watch this land
with all my fierce grief
intact. There are places that nobody
comes near without starting to weep.

Those places are mine, and they weep
the tears that I have shed. Ghosts, dreams
chase all climbers down, embodying
my faith. They sense me in the stone
beneath their feet and know what grief
floods and floods this land.

BELLS OFF SAN SALVADOR

Between waves the engine seemed to pause
and, suddenly quiet, we heard bells
ringing across the water.
For the next half hour we stood by the rail

and listened for their sound to come again
above the beat of the propellor.
Our escort had long ago turned back,
no other ship shared our visible square

of water, and El Salvador
had faded to a smoky line of land
we were waiting to forget, but the bells
pealed around us, as if a city rose

with all its noise and life, invisible
among the waves beside the freighter.
A sailor mentioned an old legend
of a city sunk in the Pacific,

but we paid him no mind. We remembered
the wharf where we had set our cargo down
crowded with longshoremen. And soldiers,
whose helmets sparkled in the sunlight.

All we knew was that cranes had hoisted
the crates onto military trucks, that guardsmen
had driven them off. The bells sounded clear
and close as voices across open water

when it is still, and the listener hears
every word of someone's private conversation.

We should not have listened, the bells
called to someone else. The ship kept going,

the sound faded, and all hands returned
to duty or to rest. Someone said it
that evening on watch, we should never
have gone to that country at all.

MEDITATION ON TV

I watch while once, twice, three times
they knock her to the ground.
Whatever she knows, she alone will know.
I want to reach into the picture

to push my hands through the electronic
blur until its sting runs up my forearms
like the needles of sleep coming undone,
wanting this to be illusion, knowing

this is how it feels to come fully awake.
My arms will emerge covered
with foreign blood. All over the world
tonight people are falling. Perpetual,

the picture creeps by. I remember watching
astronauts turn in space, the blue globe
beneath them. In space one can only fall.
One is always falling. They moved

as though it were an invention, each step
the one that might last forever.
One minute it is your livingroom, the next
a jungle hamlet. A small house

sags before you. One wall gone,
the roof folds inward with a sigh.
The family's belongings litter the yard.
Among crates, shoes, cooking utensils

I try to shake myself awake, longing
for deep space, to step once into the heavens.

THE ROAD FROM INCH'ŎN

I wade across a field that stinks of nightsoil.
Rice shoots grow up between my toes.
Minnows. Young carp that thrive
in water thick with marsh and mud.

The fields are flooded. All summer
we will keep them full, walking up the wooden
paddles of the irrigation wheel.
My feet blister and crack.

The others show me their calluses, thick
as pebbles. We climb the wheel
and water rushes among the thin stalks.
They bend as if wind, a hand,

were stroking them lightly.
We bend among the pale shoots
with water lapping the backs of our calves.
Silt catches in the hairs on our legs.

Above the road columns of dust lift
in the wake of trucks. Their motors hum,
but we hear them, like airplanes, only after they pass.
The women show me what to do.

THE COLORS OF MOURNING

The crazy people all wore black
and lived in their own section of the city.
But that was before we got there,
my mother leading her four children
out of the stuffy chill of the plane
into a wall of heat and smells, like none
we'd ever known. My father met us
with a Jeep and a strange man to drive us home.
By then the wild people — whose clothes
were not the whites of mourning —
had been taken away. New squatters
had taken over that part of town, constructing
their shanties of straw matting, corrugated iron,
and cast-off soda cans beaten flat
and soldered into walls and roofs.
Sometimes we'd see a boy riding a bicycle
with a tower of cans bound together and perched
behind him, or a man pedalling to market
toting a drunken, unconscious pig.
                    Driving through heavy rain
twenty miles south of Seoul, we passed
a skinny naked man walking in the middle of the road.
His hair plastered down on his forehead,
he wore a thin black belt.
He may have been the first naked man I ever saw,
beside my father and my brother, but then only at night
skinnydipping in the pond in New Hampshire.
For night swims we had gone naked,
shivery, and white into the black still water.
The man on the road near Suwŏn stalked stiff-legged,
his legs held far apart and his knees akimbo.
Even though it was July and mid-day,
I thought, *he must be cold.* I did not look
at his genitals, but at the black leather belt.

SUNSET OVER THE YELLOW SEA

Taech'ŏn Beach, South Korea, 1967

I watched my shadow swimming on the bottom.
Red snappers finned among the rocks.
Approaching shore, my double grew closer
and more exact. I didn't change color,
though the sea changed and looked like mustard.

In Taech'ŏn we listened at night
to voices on the radio speaking in Chinese.
I wondered how their words fit together.
They lived in another world
marked off by the DMZ, by the troops,
by our word for them, *hordes.*

One night the sun changed shapes as it set.
It became a pyramid, a diamond, then blinked out,
one last point of light holding in the sky
after the rest had gone.
The sea was still there
and the islands, black logs upon it.
I thought, China is West
through that hole in the sky.

Blond-haired girls,
every time our family drove into a village
the Jeep was surrounded by children.
Old women touched our hair.
Ipumnida, pretty.
The U.S. was living in another day
and California was East — which had always been
the farthest West you could go.

Somewhere I had a twin
who could answer my questions.
Long-lost sister, spirited replica,
she walked the exact opposite side of the globe.
Gravity was a fake; the two of us
held each other down, magnets.

THE WOMEN DIVERS OF CHEJU-DO

Cheju Island, South Korea, 1967

Only women dive, the tradition passing
from mother to daughter. It is said
men cannot stand the cold. Some divers
stay under so long I get scared

they won't come up. Blue-green balls mark them.
From the glass buoys each woman hangs a string net
to hold her catch — shellfish, abalone.
Underwater, they grab what they can

before their breath gives out.
A few of them swim ashore to rest beside a fire.
No photographs, they shout, as my father starts
to lift his camera, *unless you pay*.

They laugh as he puts the cap back on the lens.
Unnoticed, I take a picture anyways.
My camera fits in my palm. Feeling like a spy,
I snap it from waist height. My brother watches

out of the corner of his eye. At an angle
the photograph catches a cliff: the women stand
in a corner; shirtless, they have white cloths
around their heads and welts on their arms and legs.

. . .

Walking along the shore we hear a drum,
though among the big rocks we see no one.
Rounding a boulder, my mother and I nearly walk

right into a group of people. Clustered in a hollow,
they ignore us. At the center a woman dances.
We back away and watch a little from a distance.
An exorcism, my mother whispers.
See, the shaman is the man playing the drum.

                • • •

I imagine that the dancer is a diver
who has met with some evil spirit of the sea.
Her friends and family gather to help her
dance the demon out.
                As she whirls
her strength returns. Her friends grow tired,
but she does not stop. The drum sounds
as steady as the surf.
                That night the surf
becomes a drum which I dream in sound.
The group remains on the beach
while the diver dances.
                They have lit a fire
and her brilliant dress flashes in its light.

From the sea the women divers come
with string bags hung from their belts.
They dry their kerchiefs, fanning the flames,
and beside the shaman lay their prizes down.

Stars Sleep on Cheju Island

Stars move, I am bone-tired.
— Chŏng Chi-yong

I move down a slope of flowers
They tire me out
I am weary of their voices

Like children they do not tire
I am ready
to sleep among the stalks

I have walked far today
climbing up the side of the volcano
Stars move now among the flowers

Cattle graze in the bowl of grass below
They are dim hulks
boulders dotting the lakeshore

White goats descend from the heights
Bleating
they roam among the stillness of cows

White Deer Lake is the color of topaz
smoky yet clear
Goats crowd around it

White patches dance upon the shore
and constellations move in the center of the lake
The stars have walked a long way

They pause in the crater of this old volcano
softened by dark grasses
I do not tire of watching

Though heavy with sleep
I call their names and follow
They move among the cattle and do not turn

Talking to one another
they bow their heads
I fall asleep at their feet

THREE

LADDERS

I plunge in, thinking water
is not my element. I plunge in,
thinking of soldiers
who throw down their guns.
I may not pull this off: the girl's head
vanishes a second time. She is fighting
and keeps fighting when I reach her.
She grabs my collar and pulls us both down.
At four I, too, went under
with Mary's adult hand
pushing down on the back of my head.
"You've got to learn," she said.
Pressing the child towards the air,
I kick up.
I turn her over and tow her backwards.
Now I dream about ladders.
They disappear, yanked out of reach.
They peel away from docks,
falling with me into the water.
They come out of nowhere —
aluminum, wood, rope.
Painters climb into skies of paint.
Divers rise, rung by rung,
out of the awkward blue.

ON LAKEVIEW AVENUE

You were the kid who watched herself
eating dinner in the silver side of the toaster
and your father said stop that and say something.

You were the kid who played in Fremont Park
until after seven, your white tee-shirt glowing.
Your long legs carried you through the trees.

Your sister kept plastic horses on her windowsill.
Twice you put your hand through the glass of our
    front door,
you dashed your chin wide open on a diving board.

Behind your parents' house you set fire to the leaves.
The fire truck arrived red and flashing.
From outside I heard your father hitting you.

Sometimes we would stay up in the pine tree for hours.
We dug holes and covered them with boards and branches.
Always going deeper than the last time, to China.

The earth got cooler and we had to cut
through roots and pry out stones.
You were the kid with mud-colored eyes.

RED EYES AND TEETH

We wait outside the old woman's house.
Passing headlights stumble
against the tree trunks like drunks.
When it's dark again I find the other kids
by the red points of their cigarettes
floating behind the bushes.
This lady is crazy.
We have waited here before
for her to show herself, or do something.
She knows and watches us from a third-floor window,
one darker shadow than the rest.

. . .

We inhabit the nooks and crannies of town,
the iron shelves of rock above the tracks,
the brick kiln, now grown over.
In its tunnels we stash candles that disappear.
We blame the rats and try not to think
about their red eyes and teeth.
We sneak up to the places the older kids go to fuck.
When they're there, we take off (sometimes
turn to watch from a safe distance).

. . .

My breath scurries against my ribs.
Janine and I lie in the field near the marsh.
Above us sumac, berries red as lipstick,
beside us the warm brick
of the railway power station.
It hums inside.
I catch my breath bit by bit.
On the street we hear a car,
we slouch down lower and wait.

THE LOCKER ROOM

Everywhere else we wrapped our bodies
tight in corduroy, down, and wool,
but there we took our clothes off
and walked about in the humid
sweaty warmth with its faint sting
of chlorine. At first,
eighteen, a bit shocked
and shy, I carried my towel
in front of me to the showers,
not quite willing
to go covered or uncovered.
There was always some naked woman
walking from the sauna to her locker,
matter of fact, as if she were out
running an errand, though I never saw
those women buying perfume
or tampax, or crossing campus
with their files and books.
Coming in from the stiff cold
of January and of the men who did not want us
in their college, we crossed
a glassed-in bridge above the two blue pools
where the men's team practiced, their clean
thin bodies plying between the walls
on a bead above the black racing lines.
Inside the door of our locker room
heat knocked us woozy,
as we started to strip down.

LETTER TO MY DAUGHTER

Tonight I overheard someone say,
I am waiting for Nixon to die,
and I thought that he could
wait forever.
I cannot wait for you.
We have thought up names:
Rebecca, Melissa.
I would have held out for Esther.
I can hardly guess
what you might have been like.
Would you come, bold or shy, with your nightmares
and smelling our mutual sleep
to climb into the bed between us?
I dream of you nights and wake
with a tingling on my arm,
as if your hand had rested there
the second before I woke. I do not turn,
as I have for years, with my bad dreams
to the one who sleeps beside me,
but hold them to myself.

MY BONES SING

for Frances Anderson Mitchell, 1927–1961

One afternoon I notice the funny bone
glints through my skin, a pale fish
rising through water.
                                    I can't help myself,
amazed by the novelty of it and scared, I show
my nine-year-old-daughter. By now, she must
be used to such things, the dark blooms
in my fragile flesh.
                                    Sometimes I find
my changed body beautiful, — the way the organs
swell in the dim radiographs,
as if, though adult, I still
could grow.
                        The puppy my husband and I gave
the girls, after the old Airedale had to go,
knocks me down, stripping the skin
from my shins. I watch as the two of them
see me fall.
                        Both are scared
of their own small cuts and splinters;
they scream over nothing. But when I try
to hide, crying, they find me.
Their small hands gingerly pat my arms
and, even though it hurts, I accept
their comforts.
                        They pursue me into town,
so they can carry the groceries, medicines,
and cosmetics home. When I step
from the curb, they watch my foot descend,
until the sole of my shoe is flat and firm
upon the asphalt.

           On Wednesdays
the youngest comes with me to the doctor's.
When I leave her in the waiting room,
short legs still not touching
the floor and hands folded
in her lap, she eyes me.
                        Her eyes say,
you're mine. When I come back out,
her head is bent over a *Life* magazine.
She inspects each photograph,
as if through a magnifying glass.
I touch her soft hair.
                        Flushed,
she glances up. I want to take her
in my arms and carry her away,
but my skin jumps with pain and
my bones sing. She tells me
about the pictures, as we pick our way
the four blocks home.
                        The sidewalks
are papered with maple wings,
which she twirls from her small hands.
Stopped beneath one of the trees,
I start to hear a radio — Glenn Miller,
then Benny Goodman;
                        I keep hearing things
I shouldn't: words the doctors
do not use, my husband's secret relief
that it might be over. My heart quivers
in its place and pushes against my ribs.

PINE DOWN

This forest thigh bone, white pine,
lies with its old needles,
the startings of blackened loam.

Darker rings line the pith.
Your fingertips
roam across damp wood, freshcut,
to the seedling circle
they move inward.

Growing seasons,
the width of ring-years,
all the particulars we still recall,
screened in the porch together.
There were years when rain
ached to fall,
and the flush times.

There are rings in our bodies,
the stretches of what was:
the durations
we outwaited or outgrew.
At the center I reach
for the dark spot.

KUDZU

The house dreams its own demise:
vines growing faster than hands
can cast them off;
the site rumpled, like fur

on an old cat, with green.
My grandmother is painting sounds.
She stops her brush, mid-stroke,
and listens.

The house speaks differently
than it used to (no longer
just the groan of wood settling).
The muted light of the hallway

turns the exact color
she was expecting, and
in the walls the kudzu sounds
like water. She knows

it can alter landscapes faster
than any native plant
and wonders
if her brush will keep up.

BABOON HEART

Inside the gourd of the baby's chest, now stapled shut,
my ghost arms rustle and push towards the voices.
Across the room the nurses sing to her
their dreams of babies rocked

in the boughs of great mothers.
I cling to her ribs, while their song
fills the hole inside me.
She lies in her clear plastic cradle —

strung with tubes and wires, so that no one
can pick her up, small chest
laboring to keep the life inside.
Her body folds inward towards the spot

where her heart was,
and my borrowed heart, by some law
of the body's wild, confined arithmetic
grows back into a whole baboon.

I moan inside her, until I fear I will split her
wide open with my green yearning.

FAGGOTS

My lover says sometimes
that I look like a faggot, meaning
like a man
who looks like a woman.
On the dark street a woman veers away from me
and walks faster. Hands jammed
in my pockets and fast-moving,
I am also trying to stay safe

in my city at night. Like a child
I want to protest, I'm a girl —
over and over — to this woman,
to my father's two friends in the hardware store.
They said they'd have to see me throw
before they'd believe me, but I knew
that I threw just like a boy.
Coming up behind me, my lover teases,

you swish, as if I had to
pretend to walk like a woman,
or it were something I could mimic, like a man.
Like her I love the way faggots move;
I love the humor in their eyes,
their wrists, their chins,
as if their bodies kept faith
with the fire of laughter and repeated

some old joke the world could never get.
Queens are men
who leave their names behind
with all their reasons as delicate
as the works in the heart
of a watch. Robert
becomes Robin, or someone more
extravagant, more vulnerable still.

FROM A WATERCOLOR BY PISSARRO

beside a row of trees she moves
the color of suggestion
walking downhill
at evening
her basket emptied
she directs her footsteps home
still smelling the mix of
vegetable and animal
the new loaves
from the next stall
she pauses by a stream
to wash her hands
the color seems to
run from them
swirl over the stones
she holds them up
clear to the light

DEER AT NIGHT

Delicate as deer grazing, you walk your tongue across
my skin. The inside of your mouth is soft. I see a
doe, eyes broad and astonished, as we face each other
in the midnight forest. I lean into the dark of a
beech tree, she stands under thin white leaves. Among
the twigs and pine needles I lie down with you. The
smells of dirt and resin wrap themselves around us.
With my lips I touch your neck, smooth as the rock at
the bottom of a brook. You grip my fingers inside you
and I feel you pouring past — water, muscle, and stone.
The deer lowers her head to drink. One slim ear is
ragged at the tip. When she leaves, I move with her
up the bank. And in the morning I search for prints:
the hoof pressed like two fingers in the mud.

NOCTURNE

You lie all over me arm stomach breast leg and more
      your skin has always reminded me of fine sand Plum
Island a barrier beach named for its hue plum the
color and touch of your skin sleeping with the window
      open onto an orchard rows and rows of fruit trees
   the summer sun soaked and eaten up the fruit at night
still warm to the touch my window opens onto the street
      other houses spilling down the hill around us and
   behind the house a parking lot a restaurant the avenue
at one and two in the morning lovers quarrel as they
      leave the restaurant for home swearing they never
   slept with the person drunk tired is this any way to
talk about love streets quarrels fruit sand   .

IMMIGRANTS

Your skin is a country
I have learned to inhabit.
It has taken years to trust
that this new land
will not pitch and lean away.
It takes faith.
I can only be in one place
at a time, and am unwilling
to go back to the old country.

We scarcely discuss the passage
anymore: the closeness
of the hold, the stench of sweat.
Now we've changed to match
the land itself,
its roughness
and splendid gentleness.
This choice holds so few
vestiges of our pasts,
that even if you choose to leave
there will be reasons for you
to do what you must.
The ground will not drop away,
nor become uninhabitable.

POETRY FROM ALICE JAMES BOOKS

The Calling   Tom Absher
Thirsty Day   Kathleen Aguero
In the Mother Tongue   Catherine Anderson
Personal Effects   Becker, Minton, Zuckerman
Backtalk   Robin Becker
Legacies   Suzanne E. Berger
Disciplining the Devil's Country   Carole Borges
Afterwards   Patricia Cumming
Letter from an Outlying Province   Patricia Cumming
Riding with the Fireworks   Ann Darr
ThreeSome Poems   Dobbs, Gensler, Knies
33   Marjorie Fletcher
US: Women   Marjorie Fletcher
No One Took a Country from Me   Jacqueline Frank
Forms of Conversion   Allison Funk
Natural Affinities   Erica Funkhouser
Rush to the Lake   Forrest Gander
Without Roof   Kinereth Gensler
Bonfire   Celia Gilbert
Permanent Wave   Miriam Goodman
Signal::Noise   Miriam Goodman
Romance and Capitalism at the Movies   Joan Joffe Hall
Raw Honey   Marie Harris
Making the House Fall Down   Beatrice Hawley
The Old Chore   John Hildebidle
Impossible Dreams   Pati Hill
Robeson Street   Fanny Howe
The Chicago Home   Linnea Johnson
From Room to Room   Jane Kenyon
Streets after Rain   Elizabeth Knies
Sleep Handbook   Nancy Lagomarsino
Dreaming in Color   Ruth Lepson
Falling Off the Roof   Karen Lindsey
Temper   Margo Lockwood
Black Dog   Margo Lockwood
Shrunken Planets   Robert Louthan
Animals   Alice Mattison
The Common Life   David McKain
The Canal Bed   Helena Minton
Your Skin Is a Country   Nora Mitchell
Openers   Nina Nyhart

French For Soldiers   Nina Nyhart
Night Watches: Inventions on the Life of Maria Mitchell   Carole Oles
Wolf Moon   Jean Pedrick
Pride & Splendor   Jean Pedrick
The Hardness Scale   Joyce Peseroff
Curses   Lee Rudolph
The Country Changes   Lee Rudolph
Box Poems   Willa Schneberg
Against That Time   Ron Schreiber
Moving to a New Place   Ron Schreiber
Contending with the Dark   Jeffrey Schwartz
Changing Faces   Betsy Sholl
Appalachian Winter   Betsy Sholl
Rooms Overhead   Betsy Sholl
From This Distance   Susan Snively
Deception Pass   Sue Standing
Blue Holes   Laurel Trivelpiece
Home.Deep.Blue   New and Selected Poems   Jean Valentine
The Trans-Siberian Railway   Cornelia Veenendaal
Green Shaded Lamps   Cornelia Veenendaal
Old Sheets   Larkin Warren
Tamsen Donner: a woman's journey   Ruth Whitman
Permanent Address   Ruth Whitman